R. J. (Reginald John) Campbell

The Making Of An Apostle

R. J. (Reginald John) Campbell

The Making Of An Apostle

ISBN/EAN: 9783741176340

Manufactured in Europe, USA, Canada, Australia, Japa

Cover: Foto ©Andreas Hilbeck / pixelio.de

Manufactured and distributed by brebook publishing software (www.brebook.com)

R. J. (Reginald John) Campbell

The Making Of An Apostle

THE MAKING OF AN APOSTLE.

By R. J. Campbell.

LONDON: JAMES CLARKE & CO.,
13 & 14, Fleet Street.   1898.

First Edition, October, 1898.

Contents.

	PAGE
The Making of an Apostle	1
Simon Meets with Jesus	5
The Call to Service	19
Simon's First Commission as a Preacher	32
Simon Acknowledges Jesus to be the Christ	38
Simon Peter Witnesses the Transfiguration	58
Peter Thinks his Sacrifice Complete	78
The Scene in the Upper Room ...	87
Gethsemane and After	94
The Power of the Resurrection ...	103
A New Commission	113
The Prince of the Apostles... ...	123

The Making of an Apostle.

The New Testament supplies us with little in the way of biography. Even from the Gospels themselves we do not gather much concerning the actual life of our Lord apart from His public ministry. It has been justly said that no person has ever influenced the history of the world on such a scale as Jesus of Nazareth, yet it would be impossible to write a chronological life of the Founder of Christianity. What is true of the Master is true of His followers. We know very little about the Apostles themselves; apart from their life-work of preaching Christ, the details of their circumstances and fortunes are most meagre. Yet it is worth while from such materials as we have to attempt to trace the influence of Jesus Christ upon those through whom He founded His Church upon earth. The choice of Apostles, for instance, is sometimes regarded as having been made in a very exceptional or semi-miraculous way, that Jesus summoned to His side individuals upon whom His gaze fell for the first time, and that these men forthwith became the instruments of His service. But from comparison of the Gospel narratives we discover that very interesting life-stories might be written concerning the men who stood closest to Jesus during His earthly ministry. We find, as we might have expected, that Jesus took in them an active personal interest, that their lives were shaped under His influence as clay in the hands of the potter, that He had a plan with each of them, and patiently worked at it, that He applied to them a discriminating treatment and placed upon each his own individual value. Is not the same process going forward even now? Does not the risen Lord still continue to issue His summonses to the souls of men? We feel that it were better to think so, and that He by whom the very hairs of our head are all numbered still gives to His servants in the world individual care, interest and attention, fashioning heroes and saints out of the most unpromising materials, and making apostles as in the days of old.

As an example of Jesus's ways of dealing with His servants the life of the Apostle Peter is most suggestive. In the first place, because he was admitted to be the leader of the Apostles, or at any rate occupied the position of greatest prominence amongst them, and also because we are able by the comparative method to obtain from the Gospels sufficient information for a history of his character, if not of his career during the three most formative years of his life,

I.

Simon Meets with Jesus.

WE are fortunate in possessing an account of the first occasion on which Simon, the Galilean fisherman, met with Jesus of Nazareth. We are told (John i. 35-42) that immediately after the Baptism of Jesus, and, therefore, before His public ministry began, John the Baptist made a semi-public declaration that He was the long-expected Holy One of Israel. His words, as recorded in the Fourth Gospel, are: "I knew Him not: but He that sent me to baptize with water, He said unto me,

Upon whomsoever thou shalt see the Spirit descending, and abiding upon Him, the same is He that baptizeth with the Holy Spirit. And I have seen, and have borne witness that this is the Son of God." With the exception of the mother of Jesus, John the Baptist appears to have been the only person, who, at this particular time, was perfectly convinced, without a word from Jesus Himself, that the long-expected Messiah had appeared. His declaration just quoted must have been made in the presence of a certain number of His disciples, though with what effect we are not told.

In a sense the ministry of Jesus begins with the declaration of

John, and a certain importance must therefore attach to the historicity of the account of it. If John recognised, as we are entitled to think he did, that Jesus was the very person whose advent it had been his mission to inaugurate, then Jesus's own work must in its initial stages have been greatly simplified. There could be no possibility of rivalry between the teachers, nor was there any necessity for Jesus to exactly imitate the procedure of John, and to commence unaccredited the work of evangelising an unresponsive people. John had prepared the minds of his more spiritual and earnest followers for just such a revelation as Jesus was about to give. We may say without irreverence that our Lord appropriated the results of the preaching of John. The latter beheld without jealousy or disquietude the departure of his best disciples to the side of Jesus, and his own magnanimous statement in view of this change has exalted him to a high pinnacle in the esteem of Christendom: "He must increase, but I must decrease." His work was not necessarily done when Jesus arrived upon the scene. The austere and noble-hearted prophet was still able to continue doing his best to prepare the way, to strengthen the hands of Jesus and to stir the hearts and awaken the spiritual susceptibilities of his countrymen. What a majestic self-devotion!

It is not surprising that attempts should have been made at intervals to discredit the Gospel account of the close connection between John and Jesus in doctrine and discipleship. M. Rénan,* for instance, regards the Messianic proclamation as unhistorical. He thinks the story sufficiently refuted by the fact that John afterwards sent to inquire whether Jesus really was the promised Messiah. (Matt. xi. 2 *et seq.*, Luke vii. 18 *et seq.*) John's inquiry in this case was certainly very peremptory. "Art Thou the Christ, or look we for another?" But an easy explanation is to be found in the history of the time that lies between the Messianic proclamation after the

* "Life of Jesus," p. 156.

Baptism and the date of his own arrest and imprisonment. John's idea of Messiahship did not exactly accord with that of Jesus. He was surprised to find that Jesus went on quietly preaching and healing, saying little or nothing about His own personal claims, and assuming neither state nor retinue. This course of action puzzled the fiery prophet who had foretold One mightier than himself, a Messiah who should impress the imagination of the world, and render to every man according to his deeds. Jesus's procedure disappointed, and perhaps irritated him, hence the abrupt inquiry, which seems to contradict his assurance at the outset of our Lord's ministry.

Supposing, therefore, that John really did proclaim Jesus as the Messiah, we should expect the announcement to kindle a very great interest in those who understood the Baptist best. From the first chapter of the fourth Gospel we may infer that John had a school of disciples to whom he gave esoteric teaching. These few intimates were, no doubt, eagerly anticipating the near advent of Him who should restore the kingdom to Israel. We do not know how many were included in this group of enthusiasts, but it is more than probable that all, or nearly all, of the names which formed the nucleus of Jesus's first band of disciples were originally regarded as the followers of John the Baptist. These were precisely the kind of men to whom Jesus would be drawn and upon whom He could rely for the sort of exalted disinterestedness which, in some degree at least, He required from them at the very outset of their acquaintance with Himself.

But to return to the narrative of that introduction : "On the following day," the writer of the Fourth Gospel goes on to say: "John was standing, and two of his disciples; and he looked upon Jesus as He walked, and saith, Behold, the Lamb of God! And the two disciples heard him speak, and they followed Jesus." Doubtless they were influenced to do so because of the announcement of the day before.

The disciples of John were all well aware of the fact that John was the herald of a greater to come. John's statement in regard to Jesus, therefore, which statement he now repeated to themselves alone, stimulated their eager interest, and leaving their master, they followed the Nazarene. The opportunity was an easy one; there was no crowd, John was simply talking to his two followers; Jesus was alone. The sequence of events was very simple; Jesus turned, saw them following, and asked what they sought. Their reply was the counter question, "Rabbi, where abidest Thou?" "Come," said He, "and ye shall see." "They came, therefore," continues the story, "and saw where He abode, and they stayed with Him that day; it was about the tenth hour." Here we have a complete little narrative, full of beautiful and natural suggestion. These two men evidently had a long conversation with Jesus, perhaps far into the night, nor did they leave Him the next day, save for a purpose to which we must presently refer. A sacred intimacy was begun in those hours of association with the new teacher.

"One of the two that heard Jesus speak and followed Him was Andrew, Simon Peter's brother." Who was the other? Could it be the writer of the Fourth Gospel himself, John the Divine? If so we have here the record of the beginning of a holy friendship, which so long as the Church of God lasts will be spoken of. John enjoyed the singular privilege of being "the disciple whom Jesus loved," though he was not the one chosen to lead the little band of adherents whom Jesus left behind Him. To observe this first mention of John the Divine is not a digression, for the life of the Apostle John is linked in a very special way with that of the rugged fisherman whom Jesus called to the foremost place.

Why Andrew and his brother Simon were to be found in this particular neighbourhood just now we do not know. Probably they were in Jerusalem for a special purpose, and before returning to

Galilee went to listen to John the Baptist, among whose disciples they counted themselves to be. Andrew was certainly such, though possibly his brother was not. At any rate, Andrew's first thought before returning home was to bring Simon to Jesus. The narrative continues: "He findeth first his own brother Simon, and saith unto Him, We have found the Messiah. He brought him unto Jesus." And as in the case of Nathaniel, recorded in the same chapter, Jesus seems to have anticipated an introduction. The Gospel says, "He looked upon him, and said, Thou art Simon, the son of John, thou shalt be called *Rock.*" No doubt Andrew had told Jesus the name of his brother, and also that he was going to fetch him; possibly, likewise, he had referred to his impulsive, wayward character, his instability and irresolution. All the more surprising, therefore, must have been the reception which Jesus gave to the newcomer: "Thou art Simon (whom I have been expecting). Thou shalt be called *a rock.*" Jesus looked very far ahead when He welcomed poor, impetuous Simon with such a prophecy. A *rock* was the very last thing in the world which in character he would ever be likely to resemble. The new Teacher evidently saw possibilities in him which every one, including himself, had ignored before.

This, then, is Simon's first meeting with Jesus, the commencement of a training which was to yield him a destiny that the great ones of the earth might well envy. To him it was given to see a day which many prophets and righteous men had desired to see and had not seen. In this apparently commonplace man who lived, possibly, a coarse and sinful life, Jesus had discovered, though he did not say so, save in a general prophecy, the prince of the Apostles, the leader of the Church that was to be.

II.

The Call to Service.

We may assume that Peter's acquaintance with our Lord continued for some time ere he was called to actual service. The Synoptists all refer to this call, but with certain differences in detail. Matthew's first mention of Simon (iv. 18) occurs in connection with his account of the commencement of the preaching ministry of Jesus. He tells us that after the temptation our Lord went to live in Capernaum. We know little or nothing of His movements save that He

20 THE CALL TO SERVICE.

began to preach, and that the substance of His exhortation was, "Repent, for the Kingdom of Heaven is at hand!" A great deal, however, is suggested here. Capernaum was Simon's home, and by piecing the narrative in John i. with that in Matthew iv. we are justified in thinking that after making acquaintance with Andrew and Simon in Bethabara beyond Jordan, Jesus went with them to Galilee and continued His association with them on terms of intimacy, *vide* John i. 43, John ii. *et seq.* John ii. 12. Jesus's sojourn in Capernaum was not intended to be permanent, as we see in John ii. 12. It is quite possible it was only undertaken for the sake of drawing closer the

THE CALL TO SERVICE. 21

relations between Himself and the two brothers whose acquaintance He had made through the medium of the Baptist. In Matt. iv. 18 we are informed that "walking by the sea of Galilee He saw two brethren, Simon and Andrew his brother, casting a net into the sea, for they were fishers. And He saith unto them, Come ye after Me, and I will make you fishers of men. And they straightway left the nets and followed Him."

But for the considerations presented above we might imagine that this was the first time Jesus had ever seen Peter. Mark and Luke are more explicit, Luke especially. In Mark i. 16, that is very early in this particular Gospel, we read that after John was delivered up Jesus came into Galilee. "And passing along by the Sea of Galilee, He saw Simon and Andrew the brother of Simon, casting a net into the sea, for they were fishers. And Jesus said unto them, Come ye after Me, and I will make you *to become* fishers of men." When we remember that Mark's Gospel is really Peter's own Gospel, written in all probability under his guidance, we are prepared for the early introduction of the call of the first Apostle. A previous acquaintance is clearly presumed here. Mark states with his usual simple directness and vividness, "He saw Simon." The presumption is that Simon was already well known to Jesus, and the fact that the two

THE CALL TO SERVICE. 23

brothers left their nets and followed Him is not so wonderful if we consider that their friendship with Jesus was already well established, and their belief in His authority confirmed by their increasing knowledge of Himself.

It is to Luke, however, that we must turn for a circumstantial account of the crisis so briefly referred to by Matthew and Mark. Under the guidance of Luke our conjectures as to the intercourse between Jesus and Simon become certainty. In Luke iv. 38 we are told that after preaching in the synagogue of Capernaum He entered into the house of Simon. He healed Simon's wife's mother, who was suffering from fever. This appears to have been one miracle among many of a similar kind that day; possibly the news of it went forth, "And," Luke continues, "when the sun was setting all they that had any sick with divers diseases brought them unto Him." Evidently Jesus is here a familiar guest in the house of Simon and makes it His head-quarters.

In the next chapter (Luke v. 1-11) we have Luke's account of the call to service and the circumstances which led up to it. Jesus, as an honoured guest, seems to have made use, not only of Simon's home, but of his fishing-boat. This fishing-boat on occasions supplied him with a pulpit from which He was able to address the crowds that lined the seashore. On one such occasion, when He

THE CALL TO SERVICE. 25

had finished speaking, He asked His host to put out into the deep. Simon did so, no doubt thinking that the new Teacher required to escape and rest after His long exertions. But Jesus had another motive than this. Simon had been obliged to wait His pleasure while He was preaching; he had been out the whole of the previous night plying his calling, and was, doubtless, weary and exhausted. Jesus knew all this and intended to help him. By His direction Simon let down his net for a draught, explaining, however, while he did so, that he expected no result in the day-time since he had taken nothing through the hours of darkness. He lowered the nets simply to please Jesus, to whom he had become, by this time, much attached. The result was the miraculous draught of fishes.

The effect upon Simon of this beneficent exhibition of the superhuman power of Jesus was overwhelming. His impulsive character showed itself at once. He threw himself down at the feet of his Master with the ill-considered but earnest petition born of the feeling of the moment, "Depart from me, for I am a sinful man, O Lord!"

What was the reason of this strange outburst? The miraculous draught of fishes was not of itself sufficient to account for it; it was the occasion but not the cause of Peter's action. A better way of explaining it would be to try to form a sympathetic estimate

THE CALL TO SERVICE. 27

of the working of this rude fisherman's mind under the influence of his short acquaintance with Jesus of Nazareth. Like others of his class, Simon had very likely been, until the day when Andrew introduced him to Jesus, ill-disciplined and coarse. He may have thought very little about high and holy things, and yet, as often happens in a rude but generous nature, he felt an instinctive respect for goodness whenever he saw it embodied in another. He was attracted to Jesus by Andrew's assertion that He was the Messiah. In the increasing intimacy of subsequent intercourse he must have come to feel that Jesus was the best man he had ever met. Jesus came as a benediction to Simon's home. His very presence must have stirred the better feelings latent in the boisterous fisherman's heart. Simon came to love Jesus, and listened no doubt with a simple, awe-struck interest to the words He was accustomed to address to the crowds from the vantage-ground of Simon's boat. Jesus discovered him to himself: he saw how poor and mean and unsatisfactory his own life and ideals were when compared with the character of this august stranger.

To these considerations Jesus added another. Out of pure thoughtfulness and kindness for Simon He had asked him to put out to sea and let down his nets, and poor Simon, totally unprepared for the result, now saw that in his friend and guest were combined at once marvellous goodness and marvellous power. Simon's first feeling was that he wanted to get away from Him, that he was totally unfit to be in the presence of such a Being, and, like the centurion afterwards, was not worthy that He should come under his roof. The cry, "Depart from me!" meant, doubtless, "Leave my home. Do not stay with me any more. I am unfit for such a privilege, unworthy of such companionship. Select another and a better associate, for I am a sinful man!"

We are beholden to Luke for this circumstantial account of an important event in the life of an interesting man. Some persons think that Luke has mixed up this story with the similar one recorded in John xxi. There is no need to think so, the scene ends very naturally. Matthew and Mark omit to say how it was that Jesus came to extend the call to Simon and Andrew, James and John. According to their brief statement Jesus saw them casting a net into the sea; according to Luke it was He who told them to cast that net. Simon's confession and request supplied Him with a further opportunity: "Fear not, He said, from henceforth thou shalt catch men. And when they had brought their boats to land they left all and followed Him."

We see from this beautiful sequence of dealings that Jesus bestowed much tender thought and care upon the training of the men who were to serve Him in the work of evangelising the world. His prophecy in respect to Simon at their first meeting He set Himself to fulfil. Peter was not then ready to be called, nor did Jesus call him; without explaining His meaning He uttered a prophecy in regard to Simon's future character which no one but Himself could understand. He welcomed Simon's avowal of unworthiness as the first condition toward the attainment of that character. Simon was fit to be used just in proportion as he realised his own unfitness. "I am a sinful man," was the utterance which made it possible for him to arise and become a saviour.

III.

Simon's First Commission as a Preacher.

Before long it became necessary for our Lord to make a selection from amongst the number of His disciples of those who were to represent Him and be clothed with His authority, after His visible presence was withdrawn from the infant Church. In Matthew x., Mark iii., and Luke vi., we have the Gospel accounts of the appointment of Apostles. The choice was very solemnly entered upon, the Master "continued all night in prayer to God, and when it was day He called His disciples: and He chose from them twelve, whom also He named Apostles." In this little band Simon was permitted a special prominence. In the lists severally given by the Synoptists, Simon's name is always at the head. Matthew especially opens with the distinctive words, "But first, Simon who is called Peter." Simon's precedence was evidently the wish of Jesus Himself. The twelve, moreover, accepted it without demur; Simon is almost invariably their spokesman. If ever Jesus had occasion to ask a question of all Simon usually made reply in the name of the others. The only case in which his leadership was disputed was during the rivalry with the sons of Zebedee.

To this, however, we must make reference presently.

The newly-appointed apostles were now sent forth on a preaching mission; their business was to herald the advent of Jesus Himself in the districts into which He was about to come. Their theme was to be, "The Kingdom of Heaven is at hand." Certain miraculous powers were bestowed upon them; they were to heal the sick, cleanse the lepers, raise the dead, cast out demons. They were to travel without gold or silver; they were not to take two coats or shoes or a staff, but were to trust to the hospitality of those to whom they preached. They were to regard themselves as sheep sent forth in the midst of wolves;

they were to be wise as serpents and harmless as doves. They were to expect persecution; and here their Master foreshadowed what was to take place long afterwards, namely, that they were to expect to be brought before governors and kings for His sake and for a testimony to the heathen world. They were not to be over-anxious as to the form of their message; "for," said Jesus, "it is not ye that speak, but the spirit of your Father that speaketh in you." They were not to fear opposition, they were bidden to have a high courage and a simple faith. They were to yield themselves in the most thorough obedience and submission to the Leader in whose service they were now enrolled. Jesus expected to be the supreme interest in their lives. He asked for a devotion which should shrink from no sacrifice, reaching the climax of His exhortation in the statement that "He that doth not take his cross and follow after Me is not worthy of Me. He that findeth his life shall lose it, and he that loseth his life for My sake shall find it."

This preaching journey was Simon's first trial in the work of the ministry. Jesus had not only called him, He had given him work to do. It was but a simple duty, yet the faithful discharge of this preliminary obligation was by-and-by to lead to greater things. There is no doubt that it was Jesus's intention to test in this way the men whom He had summoned to His side. This preaching tour was the humble beginning of the heroic days of the early Church.

IV.

Simon Acknowledges Jesus to be the Christ.

So far our Lord seems to have said little or nothing to His disciples in regard to His own personality. He must have had certain reasons for this course, the principal one being, no doubt, that He shrank from arousing mistaken expectations in the minds of His followers. They looked for a hero Messiah, a great liberator, a secular prince. Jesus knew from experience how extremely difficult it is to change any man's point of view, or to dislodge a prepossession from his mind, hence He preferred to allow His character to produce its own impression, and from this new standing ground to raise men's ideas of the functions of Messiah. His ministry would have been seriously maimed by any premature insistence upon His supernatural claims, indeed, the danger was on certain occasions only narrowly averted. At one time the people would have taken Him by force to make Him a king, at another time they welcomed Him to Jerusalem with hosannas. He was often addressed as the Son of David, a description applicable only to the Christ, as the ready reply of the Pharisees to His own question on a critical occasion clearly shows. "What think ye of Christ? Whose son is He?" They answered without hesitation, "The Son of David." Jesus had no wish to conceal His pretensions, but on the other hand He was careful not to arouse misconception as to His real character by declaring them. This reticence puzzled the religious leaders a good deal, as is evident from their somewhat peremptory demand, "How long dost Thou make us to doubt? If Thou art the Christ, tell us plainly."

With the disciples themselves Jesus pursued the same course, for they were liable to the same danger, the danger of misapprehending the real nature of Messiahship. How long He refrained from speaking plainly on the subject we cannot determine; but some time after the return of the Apostles from the preaching mission He thought the time had come to elicit from them a theory of His Person. One day, on His way through the villages of Cæsarea Philippi, He suddenly put to His followers the question, "Who do men say that I am?" and they answered, "Some say John the Baptist, some Elijah, and others one of the prophets." Jesus continued His interrogation by the further inquiry: "But whom say *ye* that I am?" Matthew, Mark and Luke* are all agreed that Peter furnished the desired response, "Thou art the Christ, the Son of the living God." Matthew's

* Matt. xvi. 16, Mark viii. 29, Luke ix. 20.

account is the most circumstantial and conveys most distinctly the impression that Jesus was pleased with the answer. His words of commendation to Simon on this occasion are a remarkable extension of the prophecy contained in His first greeting to him as set forth in John i. 42. Matthew's version is "Blessed art thou Simon Bar-Jona, for flesh and blood hath not revealed it unto thee, but My Father which is in heaven. And I also say unto thee that thou art Peter, and upon this rock I will build my Church, and the gates of Hades shall not prevail against it. I will give unto thee the keys of the kingdom of heaven, and whatsoever thou shalt bind on earth shall be bound in heaven;

and whatsoever thou shalt loose on earth shall be loosed in heaven."

From this point Simon the fisherman becomes merged in Peter the Apostle. His training had now reached a point when his spiritual perceptions were sharpened and his faith in Jesus had led to the ejaculation which is the fundamental article of the creed of Christendom. Jesus's reference to Simon on this occasion has advanced somewhat in fulness since the day of their first meeting. Then He had stated, "Thou *shalt be called* a rock," now He avers, "Blessed art thou. Thou hast been taught of God; thou *art* a rock, and on this rock will I build My Church." Here was a high distinction for the first apostle; a trust was committed to him, the guardianship of the newly-formed Church, and how much was involved in that he himself at this particular moment could not by any means foresee. Much discipline is yet needed ere he becomes fit to undertake the grand responsibility. Probably he does not shrink from the task, for he knows not its magnitude, neither is he modest in regard to his own qualifications for it, as will presently appear. He is to be taught by failure and humiliation that to follow Jesus is a way of the cross, that power for the duty is resident, not in Peter the Apostle but in Christ who gave the commission and in the Father who revealed to him the truth about the Son of God.

The period upon the consideration of which we have now entered was a time of spiritual ups and downs for the Apostle Peter. He seems to have been too easily elated, though as easily abased. He now began to feel his importance, and was doubtless somewhat exalted in spirit by our Lord's emphatic commendation of him in the presence of the Twelve. He had declared Jesus to be the Christ, but a Christ who learned obedience through sufferings was as yet unthinkable to him. This crude perception is the explanation of the mistake into which he immediately fell. No sooner had Jesus elicited the declaration that

He Himself was the Christ than, after charging the disciples to say nothing to any man in regard to it, He began to teach them the true nature of Messiahship. In their several accounts of what follows the Synoptists differ a little. Matthew (xvii. 21) implies that some time may have elapsed ere Jesus began to systematically instruct His disciples concerning His vocation and death. Luke (ix. 22) states that He continued at once in the same interview to prepare them for His coming humiliation, shame, and death. Luke—who, as Dr. Bruce remarks, always spares the Twelve—says nothing about any further interference of Peter in the conversation.

It is to Mark that we must turn this time for the clearest account of what took place. Peter, at any rate, never spares himself in his narrations. In chapter viii. 31, Mark tells us that after Peter's avowal, " Thou art the Christ," Jesus began to teach them that "The Son of Man must suffer many things, and be rejected by the elders and the chief priests and the scribes, and be killed, and after three days rise again." It is noteworthy that in this Gospel Peter says not a word about the extraordinary blessing and promise bestowed upon himself in consequence of his acknowledgment of the Messiahship of Jesus. He does, however, faithfully and humbly tell us of the severe rebuff he received for his presumption. He was very sorry to hear Jesus predict His own sufferings and death. Such a fate did not at all accord with Peter's idea of the destiny of the Christ. He could not understand it, and we may suppose he loved Jesus too much to be willing that He should suffer anything at all, either of humiliation, rejection or failure. He was not prepared, either, to believe that his own new primacy over the Apostles was to result in nothing better than tragedy and defeat. He clung, as we shall observe, for a long time to the notion of worldly honour and advancement. Such rewards he conceived to be in the natural order of things; they were the result of his preconception of the functions of the Christ of God.

Perhaps, too, Peter felt somewhat elated and self-important on account of the words which Jesus had just applied to him, and pluming himself upon his exceptional privilege he undertook the duty of reproving his Master. For, Mark tells us, "Peter took Him and began to rebuke Him." A severe reprimand followed. "Jesus turned about, and, seeing His disciples, rebuked Peter, and saith, Get thee behind Me, Satan, for thou mindest not the things of God but the things of men." Matthew adds that Jesus also said, "Thou art a stumbling-block unto Me." Luke kindly omits all reference to the painful moment. Thus, in the course of a few moments, Peter achieved a great spiritual success and was guilty of an unspiritual blunder— he was exalted and humiliated, commended and reproved. In after days he remembered with peculiar distinctness his lack of the true spirit at this hour, and by Mark's agency, therefore, faithfully reproduced for the Church of Christ the record of his well-deserved abasement. All three Synoptists conclude their account of this scene by repeating the great saying of Jesus: "If any man would come after Me let him deny himself and take up his cross and follow Me. For whosoever would save his life shall lose it, and whosoever shall lose his life for My sake and the Gospel's shall save it. For what doth it profit a man to gain the whole world and forfeit his life? For what should a man give in exchange for his life?" Most of us find this lesson as difficult to learn as apparently Peter did.

The singular eminence of the religion of Jesus depends upon a right apprehension of the principle just illustrated. The Christian life is and must be a *Via Crucis*, yet at the same time is the way that leadeth unto life. The principle of dying to live as enunciated by Christ differs from that of even the greatest of His predecessors in the recognition that true gladness is conditioned by self-crucifixion. Human nature has been slow to learn the lesson. The great renunciation of Gautama Buddha, for example, consisted in the repression of individuality and the destruction of the natural desires. The effect of his system was negative; the higher life was to be one of self-suppression, a very different thing, surely, from self-crucifixion. Gautama placed the ideal in ceasing to live; Christ, on the other hand, taught His followers to live more deeply, truly and grandly than before. To follow Jesus, now as always, means to feel more and not less, to add to the sum of our interests, and not to take from them, to raise the standard of our hopes, not to depress it. Like Gautama, He calls for a renunciation, but that renunciation is the gateway into larger life. The solemn gladness of Christian experience finds its parallel in no other teaching that the world has ever received. How can we be surprised that ascetics and hedonists within the bosom of the Christian Church itself have so frequently and lamentably mistaken the spirit of their Master's teaching? The ideal of Thomas à Kempis, in spite of its beauty, is no more that of Jesus than was the ideal of Gautama. How slowly men come to learn that peace and tribulation, joy and suffering, gladness and the Cross, are not incompatible, but the very conditions of each other!

Before we visit Peter with our

censures because of his unmistakable reluctance to accept Christ's vision of the cross let us give heed to ourselves. The same mistakes may take very different form. With many of us the ideal of human felicity which we call Christian is essentially Pagan. Our very thanksgivings show it. We are grateful to God for troubles averted, happiness preserved, fortune assured; we tacitly assume that the opposite of these things would have been an evil. We praise the goodness of God in shielding us from the untoward and calamitous, and though it may seem hardly worth while to say it, some naturally amiable characters with a bias toward holy things have lost their faith and lost their sweetness at one and the same time with the arrival of sorrow. Far be it from me to insist that men should cease to thank God for the sweetness and the joy of life, but if we lay the stress here and refuse to take the cross when it is presented to us we have shut ourselves off from the attainment of that highest good, which is to know the fellowship of the sufferings of Christ. "Strait is the gate and narrow is the way that leadeth unto life, and few there be that find it." If the clear truth of the necessary connection between the assumption of the cross and the attainment of true blessedness were to be grasped by those who seek to follow Christ, there would be fewer of the sad failures so frequently apparent amongst those who are disappointed with the result of their faith in God.

I do believe, what you call trust
Was self-delusion at the best: for, see!
So long as God would kindly pioneer
A path for you, and screen you from the
    world,
Procure you full exemption from man's
    lot,
Man's common hopes and fears, on the
    mere pretext
Of your engagement in His service—
    yield you
A limitless licence, make you God, in
    fact,
And turn your slave—you were content
    to say
Most courtly praises! What is it, at last,
But selfishness without example? None
Could trace God's will so plain as you,
    while yours
Remained implied in it; but now you
    fail,
And we, who prate about that Will, are
    fools!

In short, God's service is established
  here
As He determines fit, and not your way,
And this you cannot brook.*

Peter's remonstrance here is but an example of a very common human feeling in regard to the things of Christ. It exhibited a certain immaturity of character and crudeness of perception such as, in spite of his genuine affection for his Master, disqualified him at this stage from understanding Him.

* Browning, "Paracelsus."

V.

Simon Peter Witnesses the Transfiguration.

At the close of the conversation referred to above our Lord stated, "There be some here of them that stand by which shall in no wise taste of death till they see the kingdom of God come with power." About a week after this promise—Mark says "six days" and Luke "about eight days"—"Jesus took with Him Peter and James and John, and went with them to a high mountain apart by themselves, and was transfigured before them." Matthew (chapter xvii.) says that "His face did shine as the sun and his garments became white as the light." Luke beautifully states that "as he was *praying* the fashion of His countenance was altered and His raiment became white and dazzling. And behold there talked with Him two men, which were Moses and Elijah, who appeared in glory, and spake of His decease which He was about to accomplish at Jerusalem." The three Apostles were in some danger of missing the vision, for, as happened afterwards in the hour of His agony, they slept, or at least were "heavy with sleep." However, as Luke continues, "when they were fully awake they saw His glory, and the two men who stood with Him." The three Galileans were awed by the sight, and Peter in his perturbation broke out with an offer to build three tabernacles. Mark says, "He wist not what to answer, for they became sore afraid." Matthew writes that, "While He was yet speaking, behold, a bright cloud overshadowed them; and behold, a voice out of the cloud, saying, This is My beloved Son, in whom I am well pleased; hear ye Him. And when the disciples heard it, they fell on their face, and were sore afraid. And Jesus came and touched them, and said, Arise, and be not afraid. And lifting up their eyes, they saw no one, save Jesus only." In the Second Epistle of Peter (i. 16-18), we have a further account, purporting, indeed, to be the direct statement of Peter himself, in regard to this extraordinary vision. He says, "For we did not follow cunningly devised fables, when we made known unto you the power and coming of our Lord Jesus Christ, but we were eyewitnesses of His majesty. For He received from God the Father honour and glory, when there came such a voice to Him from the excellent glory, This is my beloved Son, in whom I am well pleased: and this voice we ourselves heard come out of heaven, when we were with Him in the holy mount."

As they came down from the mountain Jesus "charged them to tell no man until that He should be risen from the dead." And according to Mark, "they kept the saying, questioning among themselves what the rising again from the dead should mean." It is evident that even at this point Peter had found himself unable to realise that his Master was really to be crucified and slain.

We cannot but regret that the immediate effect of this glorious vision upon Peter and James and John seems to have been a tendency to arrogance and ambition. We have now hints about a division in the Apostolic circle between the adherents of Peter and those of James and John. Peter and the sons of Zebedee now become rivals for supremacy; they had together been witnesses

THE TRANSFIGURATION. 63

of the Transfiguration—a supposed foretaste of the earthly glory of their Master which was presently to appear. Mark is our chief authority for this supposition, and we may trust that in his account we have Peter's recollection of the true sequence of scenes and incidents. After his record of Jesus's prophecy in regard to His own death he continues, "And they came to Capernaum. And when he was in the house He asked them, What were ye reasoning in the way? But they held their peace: for they had disputed one with another in the way, who was the greatest. And He sat down and called the twelve; and He saith unto them, If any man would be first, he shall be last of all and servant of all. And He took a little child, and set him in the midst of them: and taking him in His arms, He said unto them, Whosoever shall receive one of such little children in My name, receiveth Me; and whosoever receiveth Me receiveth not Me, but Him that sent Me." Luke in fewer words confirms this story; Matthew makes a very brief reference to it, saying nothing of the dispute.

Mark and Luke add a reference to another incident which gives us a sidelight upon the then state of mind of him who came to be the "beloved disciple." "John said unto Him, Master, we saw one casting out devils in Thy name, and we forbade him, because he followeth not with us. But Jesus said unto him, Forbid him not, for he that is not against you is for you." (Mark ix. 38-40, Luke ix. 49-50.) Luke subjoins a further statement about the two sons of Zebedee which, in company with the one just mentioned, leads us to imply that the three most favoured Apostles were at this time in a state of mind in which arrogance, ambition and intolerance kept company. Jesus and His followers had been refused hospitality in a Samaritan village, and James and John asked to be allowed to emulate Elijah and call down fire from heaven to consume them. Their Master at once rebuked them, adding regretfully (for He must have seen very plainly how matters were going in His circle), "Ye know not what manner of spirit ye are of. For the Son of Man came not to destroy men's lives, but to save them." Mark (x. 35-45) relates another incident of a similar kind in which James and John made a bid for precedence, requesting on the strength of their intimacy with Him that it might be given them to sit, the one on His right hand, and the other on His left, in His Kingdom. Jesus rightly replied, "Ye know not what ye ask." Matthew (xx. 20) says that the mother of the sons of Zebedee preferred their request, and that the ten "were moved with indignation concerning the

THE TRANSFIGURATION. 67

two brethren." Jesus was very patient with them. Looking beyond their foolish desire He prophesied that they should indeed drink of His cup and be baptized with His baptism, and closed with a general exhortation to the twelve to lay aside ambition, saying, " Whosoever would be great among you shall be your minister: and whosoever would be first among you shall be servant of all. For verily the Son of Man came not to be ministered unto, but to minister, and to give His life a ransom for many." (Mark x. 43-45.)

Poor human nature! The only evident effect so far of the high privilege accorded to the three foremost apostles has been to beget rivalry and jealousy between them. The Sons of Thunder display an intolerance and self-seeking which excite the anger of the others; Peter, we may be sure, included, since Peter was the person whose primacy was threatened. Peter had not yet reached the point of willing self-abnegation—far from it, as we shall presently see. Our Lord's object-lesson by means of a little child has, as yet, no result in the character of the "Prince of the Apostles." He was not prepared to exhibit the spirit of a little child, or to conform his own disposition to the heart of a little child. He was, as yet, unable to conceive how the first could be last, or how the master of all could be servant of all. The favour shown to him by his Divine Master has hitherto served but to raise him in his own estimation. From this point we shall see that only through the experiences of humiliation and failure was Peter able to attain to the true idea of Christian service.

The point at which we have now arrived is one of the most instructive in the New Testament record of our Lord's view of true manhood. It is frequently supposed that personal ambition is an essential to the progress of society. Great thinkers, before and after Christ, have agreed in recognising that this particular passion has been an instrument in the advancement of society, and hence has served a useful purpose. Before Christ the only alternative to this view seems to have been that of the duty of quiescence, and long after Christ the same theory has been very commonly held. As examples of the former view the reader has only to call to mind the sentiment of Homer's immortal epic, or the odes of Pindar, in order to see that ambition was regarded as the motor quality of heroism. Where this selfish passion was regarded as an evil and renounced in favour of a supposedly higher theory of life, the result nearly always took the form of asceticism or withdrawal from active service in the world. No *via media* was thought of as possible between thorough-going ambition and the

> . . . fugitive and cloistered virtue,

which has exhibited to the world so different an ideal. In dreamy, mystical, Oriental cults we see this latter tendency carried to its extreme. Almost invariably the renunciation of ambition as an incentive to human action has meant the disuse of many noble human powers and gifts. So much has this been the case that even in our own day, with the Christian ideal in our possession, ambition has been regarded as an indispensable ingredient in most strenuous human efforts put forth on behalf of humanity. Edmund Burke classifies sympathy, imitation and ambition together as motors in the progress of the community.* Professor Lecky, in his great work, "The History of European Morals," seems to regard it as indispensable to a vigorous national life. This great thinker, accustomed to habits of exact observation, is, no doubt, right in the assumption that this position receives abundant confirmation in the field of history; but have we so "learned Christ"?

The fact is that in giving to the world a higher ethical ideal in regard to the sanction of service Jesus must have well understood the difficulties that lay before Him. Perhaps this is why He

* Essay on the Sublime and Beautiful. Sect. xii.

was so patient with the selfish hopes of His followers in regard to their personal preferment. He must have known that the whole trend of history was against the new teaching. It is easy for us now to say that the intrusion of self-interest in any good work vitiates its value to a great extent; but must we not reflect that we owe this conception to Christ? Society is now saturated with the ethical teaching of the Man of Nazareth. We are confronted with the observation that in its moral tendencies Society is moving toward an ideal which was exhibited to the world nearly nineteen hundred years ago. We are not reaching forward to an indeterminate something in the region of morals, we are moving toward a standard exhibited in a life. Further, it is easy for us, reading the New Testament, to hastily judge and condemn the obtuseness and unspirituality of the little band that surrounded Jesus. The arrogance of Peter and the selfish intrigues of the sons of Zebedee move us to impatience. How much worthier and kinder the attitude of our Divine Master! He knew that a moral revolution could not be effected in an hour. His object was to train the men who should transform the world. If He could possibly influence the twelve men whom His Father had given Him so that they could know what they ought to feel and do, He could afford to be content. The gates of Hades should not prevail against the advancing Gospel.

What, then, was His ideal? It was nothing less than complete renunciation of all self-interest without any diminution of energy and effort in service for the good of the world. Jesus repudiated ambition in any form as the dynamic of human aspiration and endeavour. He required from His disciples the completest self-renunciation, combined with enthusiastic self-devotion to the duty of making the world better. To give up self was not to give up service, it was simply the substitution of a higher motive for a lower. This explains in a measure why Christianity came to replace the Stoic and Epicurean philosophies. Stoicism is exhibited at its best, perhaps, in the nobly active life of the greatest of the Antonines. Its ideal was rigid devotion to duty, that of Christ was service inspired by love. Ambition is a mode of self service, yet if we may so expand the meaning as to make it include the Christian principle we might say that in the place of ambition for the sake of self Christianity substitutes ambition for the sake of God. In each case it is love for a person that supplies the motive for the highest human endeavours. But how incomparably grander and stronger is the Christian principle than that which it replaced! All useful or desirable things that men are accustomed to do for themselves Christianity requires them to do for God. When the apostles finally came to understand this new commandment their Gospel became a resistless force, and whenever since their day the Church has succeeded in doing the same Christianity has arisen in newness of life.

VI.

Peter Thinks His Sacrifice Complete.

His Consequent Expectations.

In the three synoptical Gospels we have an account of a remarkable conversation between Peter and his Lord in regard to the reward, promised to those who took service in the Kingdom of God. The occasion was one of special interest. A rich young ruler came to Jesus to ask the momentous question, "What shall I do to inherit eternal life?" The disciples appear to have been much impressed by the incident—Peter, perhaps, most of all, for in Mark's Gospel we have the best account of the matter. Jesus, he says, was attracted by the simplicity, humility and earnestness of one who certainly ran the risk of incurring odium by stooping to ask advice of the new Teacher. Peter has preserved for us in one vivid sentence something of the very aspect of the Master in His final reply, "*Jesus, looking upon him, loved him, and said unto him, 'One thing thou lackest; go, sell whatsoever thou hast and give to the poor, and thou shalt have treasure in heaven, and come, follow me.'*" This test was too much for the seeker; he turned and "went away sorrowful, for he was one that had great possessions." In the discourse that followed, the Master, doubtless in a vein of mingled sadness and solemnity, observed, "How hardly shall they that have riches enter into the Kingdom of God!" Peter accepting his Master's words in their most literal sense, in the light of the foregoing incident, spoke out in his impulsive way, "Lord, we have left all and followed Thee. What, then, shall we have?"

Two things in regard to this question have a certain significance for us. The first, Peter's inadequate sense of the extent of the renunciation he had made, and secondly, our Lord's patient and wise reply. Peter evidently considered his renunciation and that

HIS SACRIFICE COMPLETE. 81

of his companions to have been complete. They had abandoned their fishing nets, and to a certain extent their homes. They had done so on the understanding that He who summoned them was the promised Messiah and future King of Israel, and therefore would be able in the future to compensate all who associated themselves with Him to their own loss. We must not suppose that this was the leading motive which attracted Simon and the sons of Zebedee to the new Prophet, but it is very clear that after they had been associated with Jesus for some time ambitious hopes for place and power began to take possession of their hearts. Of this we have already considered an example.

Up to the present they had misapprehended the deepest principle of the Master's teaching; they felt that abandonment of their accustomed pursuits and possessions merited a present and material reward not to be long delayed. Hence Peter's question—a question which no doubt related to the expectations of his companions also. The idea of a renunciation of *themselves*, a spiritual renunciation, had not yet become clear to them. From our point of view it is surprising that they should so long have misunderstood.

Had He to whom the inquiry was addressed been as most of us are, Peter would have received another sharp rebuke. How different is Jesus's answer on this occasion from the stern, "Get thee behind me, Satan!" of a little while before! The difference is due to the fact that, in this case, Peter spoke of his own renunciation, while in the former case he had ventured to interfere with his Master's. Jesus therefore replied with a patience and kindness that were possible only to one who saw far beyond the moment. "There is no man," said He, "that hath left house or brethren or sisters or mother or father or children or lands for My sake, and for the Gospel's sake, but he shall receive a hundredfold now in this time, houses and brethren and sisters and mothers and children and lands with persecutions; and in the world to come eternal life. But many that are first shall be last, and the last first." Some have objected to the tenor of this reply, arguing that it held out false hopes to those who heard it, and that to promise such a reward was in any case to lower somewhat the ideal of service. When, however, we look forward to the noble fulfilment of the promise we cannot but think the spirit of it altogether worthy of Jesus. It is a continuance of the superhuman insight which had led Him to assert on His first meeting with Simon, "Thou shalt be called *Rock*." If Mark's Gospel is really Peter's memoirs it is probable that the story of this promise was committed to writing long after Peter had begun to recognise its meaning. He who afterwards at the Beautiful Gate of the Temple addressed the cripple who asked for money was a nobler Peter than the one who now sought a similar gift for himself. "Silver and gold have I none, but such as I have give I unto thee. In the name of Jesus Christ of Nazareth, rise up and walk." *"Such as I have!"* Who would not desire to share in a possession so rich? Silver and gold, social and political prominence, had faded into nothingness in the presence of the privilege of speaking "in the name of Jesus Christ of Nazareth."

A mortal, sin's familiar friend, doth here

Avow that he will give all earth's
    reward,
But to believe and humbly teach the
    faith,
In suffering and poverty and shame,
Only believing he is not unloved.*

* R. Browning, Pauline.

VII.

The Scene in the Upper Room.

As our Lord's earthly ministry draws to a close the spiritual history of the first Apostles reaches a crisis. The scene in the Upper Room has for us a special interest in this connection. It is recorded in all the four Gospels in such a manner as to establish its importance and historicity. As usual Peter's own account is the most vivid, but Luke supplies us with a sentence from which we learn more of the state of affairs than is given by the other three.

This is exceptional, for Luke, as a rule, idealises the Apostles. He tells us that "there arose also a contention among them which of them is accounted to be greatest." We see then that even into the Upper Room and to the last Supper had penetrated the jealousies, rivalries and ambitions of these few men who were afterwards to become heroes of the Cross. We only associate the upper room with thoughts of peace and sacredness, but here is another side of the matter. It may well be that the little meeting ended in solemnity and quietness, but it can hardly have begun so. The stamp of truth seems to rest on John's account of what took place, simply because it expresses so naturally Jesus's method of dealing with the contention which Luke says was in existence. He rose from the table and performed for His followers the ceremony their jealousy of one another had made them omit. The foot-washing may have had a direct reference to the future practice of mutual service, but it had also an immediate significance. The disciples refused to wash one another's feet, and the Lord and Master of them all undertook the duty Himself. Perhaps the change of feeling induced by this simple and lowly act made possible the beautiful utterances which only John has preserved for us (John xiii.-xvii.).

In the forefront of this discourse,

however, Jesus exchanged a few sentences of special emphasis with Peter. "Simon, Simon," He declared, "behold, Satan, asked to have you that he might sift you as wheat; but I made supplication for thee, that thy faith fail not; and do thou, when once thou hast turned again, stablish thy brethren." This statement of tender solicitude must have been called forth by His knowledge of the contention which had been taking place. Doubtless He was filled with sorrow that Peter had not yet learned the lesson of humility and self-forgetfulness. He foresaw the failure, the cowardice, the denial, but He foresaw, too, the repentance, the restoration, and the greater

Peter whose strength should lie in his humility and willingness to be led by the Spirit of God. But at this moment the very last person to see any need of such a change was Peter himself. Jesus went on to describe what in the time immediately following would happen to the little band. "All ye," He said, "shall be offended in Me this night, for it is written, Ye shall smite the Shepherd, and the sheep of the flock shall be scattered abroad." Peter instantly declared, "Though all shall be offended in Thee I will never be offended." What feelings were contending in his mind at the moment we can only conjecture. Possibly he felt a little sore at the implied rebuke contained in the foot-washing and in the prophecy of the sifting which had followed it. More probably, however, the simple affection which he really had for his Master impelled him to declare his loyalty. "Exceeding vehemently," according to his own account, he persisted, "If I must *die* with Thee I will not deny Thee." He felt it was possible that Jesus might in the coming danger need to rely upon the services of an active and courageous friend like himself. Doubtless he felt every word he said, but he also felt the importance of the assistance he could render to Jesus. It never occurred to him that Jesus had no need of his assistance. Peter needed a sharp lesson, and ere long he had it. The secret of true service consists in self-emptying. He learned the true spirit of his Master's teaching only after the utter and painful failure of his own self-confident promises. For the present Jesus's only reply was, "Verily I say unto thee, that thou, to-day, even this night, before the cock crow twice shalt deny me thrice."

VIII.

Gethsemane and After.

THE testing time was not far distant. Peter, filled with determination to show his loyalty and courage, seems to have carried away from the upper room one of two swords that had lain therein. He believed himself ready for emergencies, but failed at the very outset to give what his Master really needed. Once again we find the story told best by Peter himself. He, James and John were stationed by their Master's desire a little nearer to His person than were the others.

Most pathetically Jesus entreated their sympathy. "My soul is exceeding sorrowful even unto death. Abide ye here and watch." This, however, they proved themselves unable to do. Luke says they were "sleeping for sorrow," and most likely this is in a measure true. They could not have been indifferent to their Master's trouble. He had given them sufficient opportunity to observe His state of mind, and doubtless they had done so, and were stirred with affectionate sympathy. Nevertheless this sympathy did not go so far as to enable them to share in His vigil. Probably Peter considered himself as a guard to His person—the intensity of his Master's agony he could not understand. His emphatic promise in the upper room, however, was being badly fulfilled. Even if he were no more than a guard to Christ's person he should have kept awake. In his own account of the scene he places the emphasis on this point: "And He cometh and findeth them sleeping, and saith unto Peter, Simon, sleepest *thou?* Couldest thou not watch *one hour?* Watch and pray, that ye enter not into temptation." The implied reproach here has reference almost certainly to the vehemence of Peter's promise of superior loyalty. "Though all shall be offended yet will not I." Jesus gently reminded him of the promise, and signified that he had begun badly in the way of keeping it. The Master recognised, however, the sincerity and simple affection of the Apostle in His concluding words, "The spirit indeed is willing, but the flesh is weak."

Even while Jesus was speaking the surprise came. Judas and the rabble with swords, staves and lanterns burst into the garden. Instantly all was confusion and alarm; only Jesus remained calm and self-possessed. Judas stepped forward and kissed Him; the disciples hurried to His side, Peter drew his sword, and without waiting for explanations struck at the foremost of the advancing band. The act was one of sheer folly; it might have involved himself and his companions in one common ruin. So far from saving Jesus it was Jesus who now saved him. The Master turned hastily round and with quick gesture bade Peter restore the sword to its place, saying, "They that take the sword shall perish with the sword." The statement no doubt had immediate reference to Peter's rashness. Jesus saw that any of His disciples taken with arms in their hands would forfeit their lives. The warning did not need to be repeated; Peter's new-found courage had already deserted him. The assailants seem to have been in similar case. To save His disciples Jesus confronted them, and as He advanced they retreated, stumbling over one another, till, as John relates, they fell to the ground,

"Whom seek ye?" asked the victim of Pharisaic hate. "Jesus of Nazareth," they replied. "I am He," was the rejoinder, and then, with a thoughtfulness and love of which in this dreadful hour Jesus only seems to have been capable, He continued, "If therefore ye seek Me let these go their way." For some moments the officers hesitated; the majesty and dignity of Him whom they had come to seize cast a spell upon them; no one liked to be the first to arrest Him, and Jesus had to declare Himself a second time ere the leaders ventured to execute their commission. The moment this was done, however, "all the disciples left Him and fled,"

So far Peter's self-assertion had ended in failure, but further humiliation was yet to come. He could not bear to remain in ignorance of the fate of a Master whom he really and truly loved; so, checking his flight, when he saw the procession move off he followed it at a safe distance. His friend and partner, John, who appears to have had friends in the house of Caiaphas, obtained admission for him and he waited therein, as Matthew says, " to see the end." All his bravery had now deserted him ; he was in a strange city where men of his province were despised and ridiculed. He was only a humble fisherman, and stricken with fear by finding himself in the power of authorities ecclesiastical and secular. Humanly speaking, his next mistake was one that might have been prophesied. He was discovered and questioned; in his bewilderment and terror all the coarseness of his old Galilean life returned upon him, and, forgetful of everything but the desire of saving himself, he denied his Master, with cursing and swearing. Jesus directed upon him a second reproach, this time a mute one. He "turned and looked upon Peter," but that look was enough. It brought him to his senses, laid bare his miserable failure, ingratitude, cowardice and broken promises. He saw how completely he had fallen beneath himself by over-confidence in himself. The

Peter of that moment was not the real Peter, after all. He did love his Master, and had run the risk of arrest and death to get near Him again, but his humiliation was complete and his self-abasement intense. "He went out and wept bitterly." Shall we say that the experience of the next few days was the greatest crisis in his career? From this depth of humiliation he rose qualified to become an ambassador and a saviour.

IX.

The Power of the Resurrection.

We know nothing of Peter's history during the anguished hours that intervened between the Crucifixion and the Resurrection, but we may believe that his shame and contrition continued until Jesus Himself breathed in his ear words of forgiveness and hope. We may infer indirectly that Peter must have been humbled by the recollection of his own self-confident boasting in the presence of the other apostles, for we find him still in association with them. The little company seems to have held together to mourn their lost Master and to assist each other with a common sympathy. That Peter must have been with them is clear from the fact that he was mentioned by name to the women who visited the tomb on the first day of the week. " Go, tell His disciples *and Peter*, He goeth before you into Galilee." When we consider that Peter still associated with those who had listened to his self-confident assumption of superiority to themselves we can discern something more than remorse in his demeanour. There is evidence of a new humility, and yet at the same time a continuance of tender affection for the Lord whom he fully believed he should never see again.

There is one incident in which Jesus was concerned after the Resurrection of which there is no record—there could be none. It is the first interview between Jesus and Peter after the Resurrection. The disciples in the upper room were informed that the Lord had appeared unto Simon. What took place at that first meeting we can never imagine; it must have been a season of such sacredness and solemnity that Peter would not be likely to say much about it to his brethren. The loving thoughtfulness of Jesus bade Him seek out His humiliated and sorrow-stricken follower that He might assure him of forgiveness and restoration.

Very intense and holy must their intercourse have been. From this moment Peter became a great and noble character; his discipline has not been for nothing, his self-seeking is at an end; ambition has no place in his mind for the future; arrogance and self-confidence thenceforth must have given place to a lowliness born of the remembrance of his cowardice and wretched failure. When in after days he wrote for the guidance of the saints he was writing from the depths of his own experience: "Yea, all of you gird yourselves with humility to serve one another, for God resisteth the proud, but giveth grace to the humble" (1 Peter v. 5).

The appearance of genuineness

rests upon this New Testament story. In its idyllic simplicity and faithfulness to the facts of human nature it stands in marked contrast to the spurious and unauthorised legends about Jesus and His Apostles with which the sub-apostolic age abounded. The Church has not lost much, in all probability, by the oblivion in which these lesser gospels have been buried. To unearth them now would, no doubt, be of service in throwing light upon critical problems in regard to the existing New Testament texts, but they could add nothing to the sweet and natural accounts of the spiritual history of the men who guided the early Church. We know Peter better from the pages of the four Gospels than we do from legendary accounts. Indirectly this faithfulness of the evangelic records is of great assistance in establishing their historicity. Nothing is concealed, or toned down, that we ought to know, nothing that would tend to represent the Apostles as superhuman or exceptional in their lofty character is thrust upon our notice; we are permitted to see Peter as he really was, a man made noble by the grace of our Lord Jesus Christ.

What he was, we are. Ambition, self-seeking, self-confidence, have throughout the history of Christendom been the most serious defects of the strongest characters. Sometimes these vices have been displayed upon a grand scale, oftener their scope has been petty and mean. The sins of the Catholic Church, as painted by a Bernard or a Catherine of Siena, are to be found in many a little Bethel in the Protestant England of our day. Simony is not unknown amongst the ministers of Christ, even in the ranks of Nonconformity. Not unfrequently these sinful tendencies are to be found allied with a true and earnest desire to serve the Master. All the same, they are a serious hindrance, not only to Christian character, but to the effect of Christian service; the spirit in which a man does his work has the profoundest influence upon the good result of that work. Where a man is sincere in his wish to do good, and yet at the same time in any degree the victim of his own self-confidence or self-seeking, he is sooner or later brought to the point where he must choose between his wish and his practice. In nearly every case the necessity for this choice is revealed to him by a sharp discipline. Peter's case is repeated again and again in the lives of the servants of God. It is hard to dislodge self from its vantage-ground in the region of human motives. It would be hard to find a church in which selfishness or jealousy had neither place nor influence, and it is uncommonly difficult, even for a good and true man, not to feel elated by

THE RESURRECTION. 111

admiration or depressed by being surpassed. But surely the cure for this kind of feeling is included in the very nature of Christian service. There is absolutely no relation between moral excellence and worldly recognition of it. We have conceded something to the world when we stop to think of its applause as an object of desire. It is easier to go without such applause and to labour in obscurity than it is to remain unaffected by it once it has been bestowed. Still harder is it for a man to retire from a position and a duty in which he has done nobly and well, and then to see his bishopric taken by another. Sooner or later this experience falls to the lot of most of God's heroes; it were well, therefore, that they should recognise it in advance, count the cost, know their own minds, and render unnecessary the sharp discipline which accompanies self-discovery. When God means to use us, as He meant to use Peter, He never spares us. Jesus could not afford to allow Peter to go his own way, and therefore it was that the prince of the Apostles became an instrument for good, yet so as by fire.

X.

A New Commission.

ALTHOUGH, however, our Lord had in such a beautiful and thoughtful way restored His poor, self-abased disciple in private, Peter had still a necessary discipline to undergo. He had sinned in the presence of others, it was necessary that others should know of the new understanding between his Master and himself. Only John has preserved the record of the conversation in which this new understanding was declared. But Peter himself distinctly refers to it in his Second Epistle (i., 14). John tells us in the last chapter of his Gospel that Peter and a few of the accustomed circle went fishing on the Lake of Tiberias. Peter's announcement, "I go a fishing," has sometimes been taken to imply that he had determined to renounce apostleship and return to his old life, that, in short, he was disappointed with the reward of following Jesus and disenchanted with the vision of a Kingdom of God. "I go a fishing," therefore, has been construed to mean "I abandon these dreams; they have brought me no advantage; I will go back to my fisherman's boat and my fisherman's home." It is difficult to see what justification there is for this theory. Peter was simply continuing habits he had never entirely renounced. Neither he nor John had any intention of dismissing all thought of Jesus or of abandoning His service when they entered upon this particular fishing expedition. On the contrary, it is probable that their minds, hearts and conversation were full of the marvels which had occurred since first the vision of angels had informed them that Jesus was alive. No doubt they were full of expectancy in regard to the place and time of His next appearance. About daybreak, as they drew near to the shore, they perceived some one standing on the beach whom presently they made out to be the Lord. John was the first to recognise Him, and told Peter, who instantly leaped into the sea and went to Him. Jesus had prepared a meal for the hungry disciples, and waited till they had broken their fast before entering upon the serious subject which occupied His mind and, perhaps, Peter's.

Possibly Peter had some knowledge of what Jesus intended to say, though not of the form in which it was to be said. In the previous and more private interview the Master had most likely signified to the disciple that the protestations he had made in the presence of others in the upper room would have to be referred to again in the presence of some at least of those who had first heard them. He could not, therefore, have been surprised at the three questions now addressed to him. "Simon, son of John," said the Master, "lovest thou Me more than these (ἀγαπάω)?" The now humbled Simon replied in lowly terms by appealing to Jesus's personal knowledge of him, and in particular, perhaps, to their previous private conversation. "Yea, Lord," said he, "Thou knowest that I love Thee" (φιλῶ). The reference to the upper room is distinctly seen both in question and answer. In the former case Simon had claimed for himself a superiority in devotion. He had offered to his Master the loyalty of a soldier to his captain or of a friend to his friend. He had assumed that his assistance was of importance to Jesus; he had offered to devote himself as a patriot might to his country, or a hero to a cause. Of this Jesus now reminded him by the use of a single word (ἀγαπᾷς). The English New Testament rendering of this passage fails to convey its full significance. Peter surrendered his whole position; he had no intention of doing more than affirming what Christ already knew, that even in the midst of his boasting, desertion and denial, he had very really and truly loved his Master with a deep and tender affection. This he expressed in his careful answer by the use of

A NEW COMMISSION. 119

the word φιλῶ.* In effect, he now offers the love that a child might give to a parent. He is conscious he can confer no benefit upon Christ, nor be of any service to Him beyond the powers of other people. Very humbly, therefore, he asserts that his heart is true. He loves his Master, and his Master knows it.

Three times does Jesus put the same question, on each occasion following up the answer by giving to Peter a new and glorious commission. He was to feed the lambs and tend the sheep. As

* In whatever language they were originally spoken there is a presumption amounting to certainty that the careful use of these words in the Greek of John's Gospel corresponded to the shade of meaning employed both by Jesus and Peter.

Peter had denied Him three times so now he is interrogated three times concerning his loyalty. The third test was the closest. Jesus takes up Peter's own word, and asks him "$\phi\iota\lambda\epsilon\hat{\iota}\varsigma\ \mu\epsilon$." The narrative goes on to say that Peter was grieved because he was asked the third time "Lovest thou Me?" Here we see, however, that the source of his sorrow was that Jesus should appear to doubt his humble use of the humblest word he could find to express his unchanging affection for the Master who had restored him to his better self. Jesus had pressed the question home by adopting Peter's word, and the earnest reply which followed satisfied Him. "Yea, Lord," said poor Simon,

A NEW COMMISSION. 121

"Thou knowest all things; Thou knowest that I love Thee." Then said Jesus, "Feed my sheep." Peter, though he hardly knew it, was now more ready for service than he had ever been before. Christ had accepted the service of one who now rated his own value so low. From henceforth, indeed, he was to be a fisher of men. It had taken a long time to lead Peter to this point, yet Jesus had foreseen it at their first meeting in Bethabara beyond Jordan. Very patiently had He trained him from the hour in which, with prophetic insight, He had said, "I will make you *to become* a fisher of men." Now indeed He could set him to work. Now

He could trust him with the sublime duty of being the rock on which the new-born Church should rest.

XI.

The Prince of the Apostles.

JESUS's closing words to Peter as we have them in the 21st of St. John could only have been spoken to one who had advanced far beyond the point at which ease, honour or riches were regarded as motives for service in the Kingdom of God. What a contrast between the Peter who inquired, "What shall we have therefore?" and the Peter to whom the solemn assertion was made, "Verily, verily, I say unto thee, when thou wast young thou girdedst thyself, and walkedst whither thou wouldest: but when thou shalt be old, thou shalt stretch forth thy hands, and another shall gird thee, and carry thee whither thou wouldest not. Now this He spake, signifying by what manner of death he should glorify God. And when He had spoken this, He saith unto him, Follow Me." Here again is a distinct reference to the "Lo, we have left all and followed Thee" of an earlier day. Peter is now informed that he is to expect stripes, imprisonment, martyrdom. He is to glorify God in sufferings and death. He can be under no further misapprehension as to the meaning of Christ's mission and work for and amongst men. "Follow Me!" meant more now than it had done the first time he heard it by the Lake of Galilee. Calvary had supplied the interpretation. Peter's new commission began at the Cross. Prominence in the Kingdom had been given to him, but that prominence was a prominence of suffering. He was to be first of all, not in ease, reputation or power, but first in the difficulties, the dangers and trials of the little community he had now to shepherd. In the Second Epistle of Peter i. 14, there is a pathetic confirmation in Peter's own words of the solemn charge addressed to him by the Lake of Tiberias: "I think it right, as long as I am in this tabernacle, to stir you up by putting you in remembrance; knowing that the putting off of my tabernacle cometh swiftly, even as our Lord Jesus Christ signified unto me. Yea, I will give diligence that at every time ye may be able after my decease to call these things to remembrance."

One or two instances might here be cited as evidence of the new spirit which animated him who was now prince of the Apostles. In John xxi. 20-23 we have given to us in a few words the earliest instance of Peter's new-found desire of self-abnegation. "Peter, turning about, seeth the disciple whom Jesus loved following. . . . Peter therefore seeing him saith to Jesus, Lord, and what shall this man do? Jesus saith unto him, If I will that he tarry till I come, what is that to thee? Follow thou Me." Curiously enough, this incident has been variously misinterpreted. Peter has been accused of idle curiosity or of semi-discontent at the comparison of his own hard lot with the probable happier fortune of the Apostle John.* The reply of Jesus to the inquiry has therefore been represented as a sharp and well-deserved rebuke. It can hardly be that any of these explanations represent the true state of the case. The truth would rather seem to be that Peter shrank from the new responsibility and prominence which had been assigned to him, and

* Bruce, "Training of the Twelve," p. 511.

would willingly have become a follower of his old rival, now his companion and friend. John was the disciple who understood his Master most nearly—the one "whom Jesus loved." He had been present with Peter on the Mount of Transfiguration, in Gethsemane and in the house of Caiaphas. Peter in old days had been jealous of him, and this jealousy had led to strife among the disciples. He was in no mood to strive for preference now. The disciple whom Jesus loved had, he thought, a better right to tend the sheep and feed the lambs than he had. John was the only one who had not entirely abandoned his Master; he had followed Him to the midnight trial, he had been present at the Crucifixion, and been the recipient of a pathetic commission thereat—namely, to take care of Jesus's mother. Peter now felt that John was a worthier leader of the Apostolic Church than he himself could hope to be. No doubt the arrest of Jesus had drawn them more closely together. John had done him the service of obtaining his admission to the house of Caiaphas. He had remained with him most likely in the dark hours before the resurrection morning; he accompanied him to the tomb; he was with him now. How could Peter better exemplify his humility than by his unwillingness to take precedence of a man whose true nobility and generosity he had now proved to the full? Jesus's answer gave in very brief terms a forecast of John's function in the Kingdom, and re-emphasized for Peter the importance of unquestioning obedience. He said, in effect: John's commission will not affect yours. I have chosen. Suppose that yours is to strive and lead, and his to stand and wait? How will his commission affect the faithful discharge of yours?

How thoroughly both Peter and John accepted the positions allocated to them their immediate after history shows. Peter led the van, John served in silence. Their friendship continued and expanded. For the future we hear much of "Peter and John." These two began a new friendship. John shared in Peter's punishment; if Peter did the speaking alone, John took the imprisonments with him. As they had been together on the Mount of Transfiguration, together in Gethsemane, together in the hall of Caiaphas, so now they remained together in spirit until the day of Peter's martyrdom came. (Acts iii. 1–iv.)

In a certain sense we have now reached the beginning rather than the end of the life and work of the Apostle Peter. From the point at which most of the particulars regarding his personality cease to be afforded in the New Testament commences the astonishing work of which he was in a sense the leader and inspiration. A few

Galilean fishermen set to work to turn the world upside down. The vast and venerable fabric of the Christian Church reposes upon such foundations as we have considered. This revolution wrought in the history of the world is a moral miracle. The task essayed was stupendous. Neither Peter nor his companions could have estimated its magnitude or foreseen its triumph. That he himself should come to be regarded as the first and greatest of the long line of sovereign pontiffs of the Roman Church we may be sure never occurred to him. He entered upon his task in faith, leaving results to the great Master whom He served. Compared with the great Apostle of the Gentiles he was neither wise nor learned; he was but one of the weak things of earth chosen to confound the mighty. The Holy Spirit rested upon him for service. He was a willing instrument whom God could use because self-seeking was entirely banished from his motives and desires. How this came to be so we have just seen. It was Jesus who made Peter what he was. Jesus believed in him from the first, knew him better than he knew himself, and looked to the Peter that was to be rather than the Simon that was. Jesus dealt with him in patience and love such as fills us with wonderment. Who but Jesus would have thought it worth while to do it? What He did for Simon the fisherman He is still able to do for all who yield themselves to Him. There is nothing impossible with Christ. The weakest and most sinful amongst us is of infinite value to Him. How many of us are saints in the making! May the story of His dealings with one life lead us all to the same experience of faithful and loving obedience. May it be ours to respond even through stumblings and failures to His gracious invitation, "Follow Me!" He will lead us from strength to strength, we shall learn of Him and find rest unto our souls.

LONDON:
W. SPEAIGHT AND SONS, PRINTERS,
FETTER LANE, E.C.

www.ingramcontent.com/pod-product-compliance
Lightning Source LLC
Chambersburg PA
CBHW031324160426
43196CB00007B/650